MORE Improving Comprehension

for ages 10-11

A & C Black • London

Contents

Each text has three comprehension exercises to enable teachers to differentiate across the ability range.

Introduction		Page 3
France	Non-fiction: Information text	Pages 5–8
French holiday	Narrative: Story with a familiar setting	Pages 9–12
Learning French	Narrative: Story with a familiar setting	Pages 13–16
Rosetta Stone	Non-fiction: Information text	Pages 17–20
Stig's house	Narrative: fantasy extract from *'Stig of the Dump'* by Clive King	Pages 21–24
Flat for sale	Non-fiction: Estate Agent details	Pages 25–28
House for sale	Non-fiction: Estate Agent details	Pages 29–32
Running for his life	Narrative: historical fantasy extract from *'Wolf Brother'* by Michelle Paver	Pages 33–36
Wolf	Non-fiction: Information text	Pages 37–40
Lone Dog by Irene McLeod	Poetry: Pattern and rhyme	Pages 41–44
William Shakespeare	Non-fiction: Biography	Pages 45–48
Macbeth	Narrative: retelling of the play, extract from *The Enchanted Island* by Ian Serraillier	Pages 49–52
Snowmen	Play script	Pages 53–56
Football practice 1	Poetry: Pattern and rhyme	Pages 57–60
Football practice 2	Poetry: Pattern and rhyme	Pages 61–64

Introduction

Following the success of the Improving Comprehension series, *More Improving Comprehension* provides a further range of interesting and exciting texts for sharing with pupils. The texts have been carefully selected to be appropriate to the age group and to cover a range of text types. The accompanying comprehension worksheets are differentiated at three levels and are designed to be used by individuals or small groups. **Notes for teachers** at the foot of each worksheet provide guidance on how to get the most from the texts and how to approach the questions on the sheet.

For monitoring and recording purposes, an **Individual Record Sheet** is provided on page 4 detailing reading and writing levels appropriate for Year 6. You may find it helpful to make indicative assessments of pupils' levels in both reading and writing by considering their responses to the comprehension exercises.

How to use the book and CD-ROM together

The book has fifteen texts, which can be projected on to a whiteboard for whole class use from the CD-ROM, or photocopied/printed for use with small groups or individuals. Sharing the text either on screen or paper provides lots of opportunities for speaking and listening, for decoding words through a phonic approach, for reading and re-reading for meaning, and for satisfaction and enjoyment in shared success.

For each text there are three comprehension worksheets at different ability levels to enable teachers to differentiate across the ability range. An animal picture at the top of the sheet indicates the level of the worksheet. The cat exercises are at the simplest level; the dog exercises are at the next level; the rabbit exercises are at the most advanced level. You may decide to give some pupils the cat worksheet and then decide, on the basis of their success, to ask them to complete the dog worksheet. A similar approach could be taken with the dog and rabbit sheets.

After reading the text with the pupils, the teacher should discuss the tasks with the children, ensuring that they understand clearly how to complete the worksheet and reminding them to answer the questions using full sentences and correct punctuation.

National Curriculum levels

The worksheets are aimed at the following ability levels:

Cat worksheets are for pupils working at Level 3.
Dog worksheets are for pupils working confidently at Level 4.
Rabbit worksheets are for pupils who are working at Level 5.

Individual record sheet

Pupil's name: _____
Date of birth: _____

Reading Level 3
- ☐ I can read a range of texts fluently and accurately.
- ☐ I can read independently.
- ☐ I use strategies appropriately to establish meaning.
- ☐ In my responses to fiction I show understanding of the main points and I express preferences.
- ☐ In my responses to non-fiction I show understanding of the main points and I express preferences.
- ☐ I know the order of the alphabet.
- ☐ I use my knowledge of the alphabet to locate books and find information.

Reading Level 4
- ☐ I can respond to a range of texts.
- ☐ I show understanding of significant ideas, themes, events and characters.
- ☐ I am beginning to use inference and deduction.
- ☐ I refer to the text when explaining my views.
- ☐ I can locate and use ideas and information.

Reading Level 5
- ☐ I can understand a range of texts.
- ☐ I can select essential points and use inference and deduction where appropriate.
- ☐ In my responses, I can identify key features, themes and characters.
- ☐ I can select sentences, phrases and relevant information to support my views.
- ☐ I can retrieve and collate information from a range of sources.

Writing Level 3
- ☐ My writing is often organised, imaginative and clear.
- ☐ I use the main features of different forms of writing.
- ☐ I am beginning to adapt my writing to different readers.
- ☐ I use sequences of sentences to extend ideas logically.
- ☐ I choose words for variety and interest.
- ☐ The basic grammatical structure of my sentences is usually correct.
- ☐ My spelling is usually accurate, including that of common, polysyllabic words.
- ☐ I use punctuation accurately to mark sentences, including full stops, capital letters and question marks.
- ☐ My handwriting is joined and legible.

Writing Level 4
- ☐ I can write in a range of forms.
- ☐ My writing is lively and thoughtful.
- ☐ My ideas are often sustained and developed in interesting ways.
- ☐ My ideas are often organised appropriately for the purpose of the reader.
- ☐ My choice of vocabulary is often adventurous.
- ☐ I use words for effect.
- ☐ I am beginning to use grammatically complex sentences to extend meaning.
- ☐ My spelling, including that of polysyllabic words that conform to regular patterns, is generally accurate.
- ☐ I use full stops, capital letters and question marks correctly.
- ☐ I am beginning to use punctuation within the sentence.
- ☐ My handwriting is fluent, joined and legible.

Writing Level 5
- ☐ My writing is varied and interesting.
- ☐ I can convey meaning clearly in a range of forms for different readers.
- ☐ I can use a more formal style where appropriate.
- ☐ My vocabulary choices are imaginative.
- ☐ I can use words precisely.
- ☐ I organise simple and complex sentences into paragraphs.
- ☐ I usually spell words with complex regular patterns correctly.
- ☐ I can usually use accurately a range of punctuation, including commas, apostrophes and inverted commas.
- ☐ My handwriting is joined, clear and fluent.
- ☐ Where appropriate, I can adapt my handwriting to a range of tasks.

France

The French Republic, better known as France, is a major European country situated to the south of the United Kingdom. At its closest point it is only twelve miles away from Kent, across the English Channel. It has borders with several countries: Belgium, Luxembourg, Germany, Switzerland, Italy, Monaco, Andorra and Spain.

France is the largest country in western Europe, with a total land area of 674,843 square kilometres, occupied by a population of about 66 million people. In comparison, our country, the United Kingdom of Great Britain and Northern Ireland, has a population of approximately 62 million people living in an area of just 243,610 square kilometres.

France is a very popular country for tourists to visit: over 82 million people visit the French Republic every year. Many people enjoy visiting Paris, the capital city, where there are famous art galleries. The Eiffel Tower can be seen from many miles away and visitors can climb to its first and second level by steps then take lifts to the third level, from which they can gain wonderful views right across the whole city. Just to the south of Paris is the very popular Disneyland Paris theme park and to the north is the Parc Asterix.

In the summer, French beaches are great attractions for visitors. The sandy beaches of Brittany in the north-west of France and of the Cote d'Azur in the south are particularly popular with tourists. In the winter, many people head for the French Alps where they can enjoy skiing in the wonderful mountain scenery.

Most tourists from the United Kingdom reach France by ferry from English ports such as Plymouth, Poole, Portsmouth and Dover, or by travelling through the Channel Tunnel. The Channel Tunnel first opened in 1994 and links Folkestone in Kent with a place called Coquelles, which is near Calais in France. Passengers can travel through the tunnel on the Eurostar train or they can take their cars on the Eurotunnel car shuttle train.

France

Name: _____ Date: _____

Answer the questions using full sentences.

1 What is another name for the country of France?
   _____
   _____

2 Which other countries are geographically joined to France?
   _____
   _____

3 How many people live in France?
   _____
   _____

4 How many people live in our country?
   _____
   _____

5 From which building would you get a good view of Paris?
   _____
   _____

6 Why might people visit France in the summer time or the winter time?
   _____
   _____
   _____
   _____

Notes for teachers
Help the children to read the passage slowly and carefully, ensuring that they understand that it is non-fiction. Discuss the questions with them and encourage them to work out their answers orally before putting anything down on paper. Do they remember to write in complete sentences, using appropriate punctuation?

Name: _____ Date: _____

France

Answer the questions using full sentences.

1 How many people visit France every year?
   _____
   _____

2 What do people like to visit in Paris?
   _____
   _____

3 Why do people like to visit the French coast?
   _____
   _____

4 How do most people travel to France from the United Kingdom?
   _____
   _____

5 Write two facts about the Channel Tunnel.
   _____
   _____

6 Would you like to visit France? Describe aspects of France that you would like to see or aspects you think you wouldn't like.
   _____
   _____
   _____
   _____
   _____

Notes for teachers
Ask the children to read the passage carefully, ensuring that they understand that it is non-fiction. Discuss the questions with them and encourage them to work out their answers orally before putting anything down on paper. Do they remember to write in complete sentences, using appropriate punctuation? Encourage them to find information from the passage to help them to answer question 6.

Andrew Brodie: More Improving Comprehension for Ages 10–11 © A&C Black, Bloomsbury Publishing 2012

France

Answer the questions using full sentences.

1 How does the population of France compare to the population of the UK?

2 How does the area of France compare to the area of the UK?

3 Why do you think tourism is important to the French Republic?

4 Where would you like to visit in France and why would you like to go there?

5 How do people travel from the UK to the French Republic? Can you think of another way that is not mentioned in the passage?

6 Find information on another country. Write five key facts about that country.

Notes for teachers
Ask the children to read the passage carefully, ensuring that they understand that it is non-fiction. Discuss the questions with them and encourage them to work out their answers orally before putting anything down on paper. Do they remember to write in complete sentences, using appropriate punctuation? Encourage them to research in books and/or on the internet to find information for question 6.

French holiday

Tom had never been to France before so he was quite excited when the family left the caravan and rushed down to the beach on the very first day of the holiday. If only he had his friends with him, he thought. Or, if only he had a brother to spend time with or even a sister.

Dad spread out the blanket on the soft sand and Mum started hammering in the poles of the wind-break. Tom knew he should be helping but he couldn't resist tearing off his clothes then struggling into his swim-shorts under his big red beach towel.

'See you later!' he called, and ran down the beach to splash into the sea. The cold of the water came as a shock to him after the feeling of the hot sand under his feet. He quickly ran back out of the water and stood staring at the sea. He might pluck up courage to go in properly in a minute, he decided.

He looked in both directions along the beach: to his left, the cliffs curved round towards the sea and there were large boulders where the sand ended. To his right, the sand stretched for a long way until meeting rocks and cliffs, which were illuminated by the bright sunlight. At that end of the beach there was a small island on top of which, a small building that could be a castle was set amongst pine trees.

Tom thought that the castle island could be worth exploring later. Perhaps the tide would go out far enough for him to be able to walk to the island. Or maybe he would just have to swim a short distance. That water was cold though!

For now, Tom turned in the other direction and ran along the sand. It was much easier to run here than further up the beach because the sand was damp and firm. Occasionally he allowed himself to run through the shallowest water where small waves were making their final approach to dry land. Tom had not felt so happy for a very long time.

French holiday

Answer the questions using full sentences.

1 Why was Tom in France?

2 What was Tom staying in when in he was in France?

3 What did Mum and Dad do when they got to the beach?

4 Why did Tom run out of the sea?

5 What could Tom see on top of a small island?

6 Write about a time when you visited a beach.

Notes for teachers
Help the children to read the passage slowly and carefully, ensuring that they understand the story. Discuss the questions with them and encourage them to work out their answers orally before putting anything down on paper. Do they remember to write in complete sentences, using appropriate punctuation? Talk through the final question: can the children remember all the things they saw and did when they visited the seaside? (If any child has not been to the seaside, ask them to talk and write about another day out they have experienced.)

French holiday

Answer the questions using full sentences.

1. At what time of the year do you think the story takes place? How do you know?

2. Why was Tom excited on the first day of the holiday?

3. Why did Tom have a shock when he went into the sea?

4. How did Tom think he could reach the castle island?

5. What type of sand did Tom find easiest to run on and why was it easier?

6. Write about a time when you went somewhere special.

Notes for teachers
Ask the children to read the passage slowly and carefully, ensuring that they understand the story. Discuss the questions with them and encourage them to work out their answers orally before putting anything down on paper. Do they remember to write in complete sentences, using appropriate punctuation? Talk through the final question: can the children remember all the things they saw and did when they had a special day out?

French holiday

Answer the questions using full sentences.

1 Tom had mixed emotions at the start of the passage. Describe how he felt.
   _____
   _____
   _____

2 How did he feel at the end of the passage and why did he feel this way?
   _____
   _____
   _____

3 Why might Tom have felt guilty when he ran down the beach?
   _____
   _____

4 What was the weather like that day and how do you know that?
   _____
   _____

5 Why did Tom turn left when he set off exploring?
   _____
   _____

6 How would you spend a perfect day?
   _____
   _____
   _____
   _____
   _____

Notes for teachers
Ask the children to read the passage carefully, ensuring that they understand the story. Discuss the questions with them and encourage them to work out their answers orally before putting anything down on paper. Do they remember to write in complete sentences, using appropriate punctuation? Talk through the final question: can the children plan what they would do?

Learning French

When he reached the end of the beach, Tom began to clamber over the rocks. At high tide the sea water had filled the nooks and hollows in the rocks, creating dozens of small pools when the sea retreated. Each rock-pool contained crystal clear water in which a variety of creatures were living.

Tom gazed into a large rock-pool, watching small fish and crabs darting amongst the sea anemones. He wished that he had a net like the one he'd had when he was younger.

"Bonjour," said a voice from behind him.

Tom looked around to see a girl of about his age, dressed in a bright yellow t-shirt and shorts. She was clutching a bucket in one hand and a fishing net in the other. "Hello," he replied.

"You are English?" asked the girl, but in a strong French accent.

"Yes," replied Tom. "You are French?" he asked, though he was sure he already knew the answer.

"Oui," replied the girl. "Je m'appelle Claire," she added.

Tom hadn't learnt any French before but he guessed that she must have just told him her name as, of course, he recognised the name 'Claire'. "I'm Tom," he said, pointing at himself.

"You must speak French!" she said in English, grinning at him.

Tom wasn't sure that he wanted to be bossed around by anybody but there was something about this girl that made him feel that he had little choice. The only problem was that he had no idea what to say or how to say it.

Seeing Tom's confusion, Claire pointed at herself and said again, "Je m'appelle Claire." Then she pointed at Tom.

He guessed that this was his cue to attempt his first ever words of French. "Je … ma … pell … Tom!" he said, slowly and carefully.

The girl smiled widely. Tom wasn't sure whether she was making fun of him or whether she was highly impressed by his brilliant French.

"Tres bon, Tom!" she said, enthusiastically.

Tom returned her smile, now convinced that she was highly impressed. He was clearly a natural at speaking French, he concluded.

Learning French

Answer the questions using full sentences.

1 What country was Tom visiting?
_____
_____

2 How had the rock-pools been created?
_____
_____

3 What could Tom see in one of the rock-pools?
_____
_____

4 What did the girl look like?
_____
_____

5 What was the girl's name?
_____
_____

6 Describe a person in your class. What does she or he look like?
_____
_____
_____
_____

Notes for teachers
Help the children to read the passage slowly and carefully, ensuring that they understand the story. Discuss the questions with them and encourage them to work out their answers orally before putting anything down on paper. Do they remember to write in complete sentences, using appropriate punctuation? Talk about the final question, helping the children to identify features of other pupils that they can describe. Obviously a clear rule must be that there should be no negative statements about the subject.

Learning French

Answer the questions using full sentences.

1. Where exactly was Tom?

2. What was strange about the word that Tom heard from behind him?

3. Write down exactly what Claire said in French to Tom. Can you translate what she said?

4. Why did Claire repeat one of her French phrases?

5. Why was Tom concerned when Claire smiled at his French?

6. Describe a person you have met. What does she or he look like?

Notes for teachers
Ask the children to read the passage slowly and carefully. Discuss the questions with them and encourage them to work out their answers orally before putting anything down on paper. Do they remember to write in complete sentences, using appropriate punctuation? Talk about the final question, helping the children to identify features of someone that they can describe. Obviously a clear rule must be that there should be no negative statements about the subject.

Andrew Brodie: More Improving Comprehension for Ages 10–11 © A&C Black, Bloomsbury Publishing 2012

Learning French

Name: _____ Date: _____

Answer the questions using full sentences.

1 Describe Claire. Think about the way she looks, the things she says, the way she makes Tom feel.
_____
_____
_____
_____
_____
_____
_____
_____
_____
_____
_____

2 Describe a person you know well, but not someone in your class.
_____
_____
_____
_____
_____
_____
_____
_____
_____
_____
_____

Notes for teachers
Ask the children to read the passage slowly and carefully. Discuss the two questions with them – encourage them to find evidence from the passage to help them to develop a description of Claire. Can they use similar evidence to describe someone they know? Do they remember to write in complete sentences, using appropriate punctuation?

16 Andrew Brodie: More Improving Comprehension for Ages 10–11 © A&C Black, Bloomsbury Publishing 2012

One of the most impressive exhibits in the British Museum is a big lump of rock! It's called the Rosetta Stone.

In the year 196 BC, the king of Egypt declared that some important writing had to be inscribed on a large rock. At first when we look at it now, the writing does not seem very exciting: much of it is a decree (an official order) about allowing priests not to pay tax. However, this becomes interesting when we discover that the decree was made by King Ptolemy the fifth who was only about fourteen years old when the decree was made. Even more interesting is the fact that Ptolemy V had already been king for nine years!

After the decree had been painstakingly carved into the rock, the stone was probably displayed in a temple. Hundreds of years later it wasn't considered important any more so it was moved and was used as part of the building material for a fort. The fort was being built near the town of Rosetta in the Nile Delta, which is why we now call the stone the Rosetta Stone.

The stone was found by French soldiers in 1799 but was captured from the French by British soldiers in 1801. It was brought to London and immediately sparked great interest. People were puzzled by the fact that the writing on the stone appeared to be in three different languages, one of which was Ancient Greek and another was Egyptian hieroglyphics. The skill of reading and understanding hieroglyphics had been lost hundreds of years earlier – it was a written language that nobody used any more.

At first nobody knew what the writing on the stone actually said but experts began to study it carefully and by 1803 the Greek section of the text had been translated. Then people realised that the other two languages contained the same information. The experts carefully matched the Greek text to the Ancient Egyptian text and slowly they began to be able to read the hieroglyphics.

The Rosetta Stone has now been displayed in the British Museum for over two hundred years. It is considered to be a most valuable object as it provided the first key to translating Ancient Egyptian hieroglyphics.

Rosetta Stone

Answer the questions using full sentences.

1 Where could you see the Rosetta Stone?

2 What is written on the Rosetta Stone?

3 When was the writing inscribed on the Stone?

4 Who found the Stone?

5 Which language was a mystery to people until the Rosetta Stone was used to translate it?

6 Write some words in a foreign language, together with the same words in English.

Notes for teachers
Help the children to read the passage slowly and carefully, ensuring that they understand the non-fiction story. Discuss the questions with them and encourage them to work out their answers orally before putting anything down on paper. Do they remember to write in complete sentences, using appropriate punctuation? Help them to answer question 6 by referring to books or the internet.

Rosetta Stone

Name: _____ Date: _____

Answer the questions using full sentences.

1 What is written on the Rosetta Stone?
   _____
   _____

2 Who decided what should be written on the Stone?
   _____
   _____

3 How old was King Ptolemy V when he became king?
   _____
   _____

4 Why were people so interested in the Stone when it was found?
   _____
   _____

5 How did people translate the hieroglyphics?
   _____
   _____

6 Write some words in a foreign language, together with the same words in English.

   _____   _____
   _____   _____
   _____   _____
   _____   _____

Notes for teachers
Ask the children to read the passage carefully, ensuring that they understand the non-fiction story. Discuss the questions with them and encourage them to work out their answers orally before putting anything down on paper. Do they remember to write in complete sentences, using appropriate punctuation? Help them to answer question 6 by referring to books or the internet.

Rosetta Stone

Answer the questions using full sentences.

1. Which king of Egypt ordered the decree to be written on the Stone?

2. In which year did he become king?

3. How many years ago was the Rosetta Stone inscription created?

4. How many years ago was the Stone found near the town of Rosetta?

5. Which two languages are mentioned in the passage? Can you find the name of the third language that was written on the Stone?

6. Write two sentences in a foreign language, together with translations of these sentences in English.

Notes for teachers
Ask the children to read the passage carefully, ensuring that they understand the non-fiction story. Discuss the questions with them and encourage them to work out their answers orally before putting anything down on paper. Do they remember to write in complete sentences, using appropriate punctuation? Help them to answer questions 5 and 6 by referring to books or the internet.

Stig's house

The extract below comes from the book 'Stig of the Dump' by Clive King. Barney has just fallen through the roof of Stig's house and has met Stig for the first time. He tries to make conversation but Stig doesn't seem to speak English.

Stig seemed to understand that Barney was approving of his home and his face lit up. He took on the air of a householder showing a visitor round his property, and began pointing out some of the things he seemed particularly proud of.

First, the plumbing. Where the water dripped through a crack in the roof of the cave he had wedged the mud-guard of a bicycle. The water ran along this, through the tube of a vacuum cleaner, and into a big can with writing on it. By the side of this was a plastic football carefully cut in half, and Stig dipped up some water and offered it to Barney. Barney had swallowed a mouthful before he made out the writing on the can: it said WEEDKILLER. However, the water only tasted of rust and rubber.

It was dark in the back of the cave. Stig went to the front where the ashes of a fire were smoking faintly, blew on them, picked up a book that lay beside his bed, tore out a page and rolled it up, lit it at the fire, and carried it to a lamp set in a niche in the wall. As it flared up Barney could see it was in fact an old teapot, filled with some kind of oil, and with a bootlace hanging out of it for a wick.

In the light of the lamp Stig went to the very back of the cave and began to thump the wall and point, and explain something in his strange grunting language. Barney did not understand a word but he recognized the tone of voice – like when grown-ups go on about: 'I'm thinking of tearing this down, and building on here, and having this done up . . .' Stig had been digging into the wall, enlarging his cave. There was a bit of an old bed he had been using as a pick, and a baby's bath full of loose chalk to be carried away.

Barney made the interested sort of noises you are supposed to make when people tell you they are going to put up plastic wallpaper with pictures of mousetraps on it, but Stig reached up to a bunch of turnips hanging from a poker stuck in the wall. He handed Barney a turnip, took one for himself, and began to eat it. Barney sat down on a bundle of old magazines done up with string and munched the turnip. The turnip at least was fresh, and it tasted better to him than the cream of spinach he'd hidden under his spoon at dinner time.

Stig's house

Answer the questions using full sentences.

1 What book does the passage come from?

2 What are the names of the two characters in the extract?

3 Which character does not speak English?

4 What could be dangerous about drinking water from the big can?

5 How was the cave lit?

6 Can you draw a sketch to show how Stig's water supply worked?

Notes for teachers
Help the children to read the passage slowly and carefully, ensuring that they understand the story. Talk about how the two characters are managing to communicate. Do the children understand how the teapot worked as a lamp? Discuss the questions with them and encourage them to work out their answers orally before putting anything down on paper. Do they remember to write in complete sentences, using appropriate punctuation? For question 6, help the children to read the 'plumbing' section of the passage as a guide for their sketch.

Stig's house

Answer the questions using full sentences.

1 Who wrote the book 'Stig of the Dump'?

2 How do we know that Stig was pleased by Barney's reaction to his home?

3 What did they use to drink from?

4 Why did Stig want to light the lamp?

5 What had Stig been doing at the back of the cave?

6 What did they eat? How would you feel about eating those?

7 What is the strangest thing you've ever eaten? Did you like it?

Notes for teachers
Ask the children to read the passage carefully, ensuring that they understand the story. Discuss the questions with them and encourage them to work out their answers orally before putting anything down on paper. Do they remember to write in complete sentences, using appropriate punctuation? Talk about question 7, which can be very challenging for some children – give them ideas, including different vegetables, fruits, desserts, etc.

Stig's house

Name: _____ Date: _____

Answer the questions using full sentences.

1 Where do you think Stig lives?
   _____
   _____

2 What did Barney think of Stig's house?
   _____
   _____

3 What should Barney have done before drinking the water?
   _____
   _____

4 What did Stig use the book and the magazines for?
   _____
   _____

5 What did Stig's tone of voice reveal?
   _____
   _____

6 Describe the strangest place you have ever visited.
   _____
   _____
   _____
   _____
   _____

Notes for teachers
Ask the children to read the passage carefully, ensuring that they understand the story. Discuss the questions with them and encourage them to work out their answers orally before putting anything down on paper. Do they remember to write in complete sentences, using appropriate punctuation? Talk about question 6, helping the children to think of ideas about homes, castles, schools, caves, forests, beaches, etc.

3 Longdown Tower, West Tunton, Bristol, BS29 4BU

A most attractive first floor flat with living/dining room, separate kitchen, bathroom, two bedrooms, gas central heating, parking space and access to communal play area.

The property
3 Longdown Tower is now in need of some modernisation but offers ample accommodation and is situated in a well maintained block of flats. It comprises:

Living/dining room (5m by 3.2m) with windows to two aspects.

Kitchen (3m by 2.4m), fitted with gas boiler, cooker and hob, washer-dryer. Generous work-tops with tiling over.

Bedroom 1 (4.1m by 3.1m) with fitted wardrobe.

Bedroom 2 (3.1m by 2.4m)

Bathroom (3.1m by 2.2m) with attractive suite comprising WC, sink and bath with shower over.

Outside, the property benefits from a single parking space and a communal grass area with some play equipment.

Directions
From our office, turn right at the traffic lights into South Street then proceed to the second mini roundabout. Take the left fork and Longdown Tower can be found on the left hand side.

Viewings
Strictly by appointment through our office, on 01964 887766

Services
We believe that the property is served by mains gas, electricity, water and drainage. Please confirm this through the vendor and your solicitor.

Price
£127500 leasehold.

Name: _____ Date: _____

Flat for sale

Ring the correct answer for each of the following three questions.

1   A person who sells flats and houses is called

    a newsagent   an estate agent   a literary agent   a travel agent

2   A flat is sometimes known as

    an apartment   a level   a bungalow   a mobile home

3   Another word for 'communal' could be

    communion   committee   share   shared

Use full sentences to answer the next questions.

4   How many bedrooms does the flat have?
_____
_____

5   Which is the biggest room in the flat?
_____
_____

6   Write a list of all the rooms in your home.
_____
_____
_____
_____
_____

Notes for teachers
Help the children to read the passage slowly and carefully, ensuring that they understand that it consists of estate agents' details about a flat that is for sale. Do they remember to write in complete sentences, using appropriate punctuation, for the final three questions? You may like to suggest that they elaborate slightly on their list for question 6 by giving a few details about some of the rooms.

Flat for sale

Name: _____ Date: _____

Ring the correct answer for each of the following three questions.

1   A word similar in meaning to 'access' is

  accent   entrance   entry   enter

2   A word similar in meaning to 'outside' is

  exterior   interior   external   internal

3   Another word for 'confirm' could be

  agreement   agreeable   aggregate   agree

Use full sentences to answer the next questions.

4   How many rooms does the flat have?

  _____
  _____

5   Do you think that the property is suitable for a family? Explain your answer.

  _____
  _____

6   Write a list of the rooms in your school.

  _____
  _____
  _____
  _____

Notes for teachers
Ask the children to read the passage carefully, ensuring that they understand that it consists of estate agents' details about a flat that is for sale. Do they remember to write in complete sentences, using appropriate punctuation, for the final three questions? Talk through question 6 with them, pointing out that there is no need to list each classroom separately but that they could instead, for example, write 6 classrooms, 2 boys' toilets, 2 girls' toilets, staffroom, etc.

Name: _____ Date: _____

Ring the correct answer for each of the following three questions.

1. A word similar in meaning to 'aspects' is

   views   opinions   expects   sides

2. A word similar in meaning to 'generous' is

   large   kind   mean   wooden

3. Another word for 'comprising' could be

   composing   composting   competing   comparing

Use full sentences to answer the next questions.

4. What sort of building is the flat in?
   _____
   _____

5. What do you think the agent means in stating that the flat is 'in need of some modernisation'?
   _____
   _____

6. The floor area of a room can be calculated by multiplying the length by the width. Using a calculator find the floor area of each room in the flat, then find the total floor area of the accommodation.
   _____
   _____
   _____
   _____
   _____

Notes for teachers
Ask the children to read the passage carefully, ensuring that they understand that it consists of estate agents' details about a flat that is for sale. Do they remember to write in complete sentences, using appropriate punctuation, for the final three questions? Talk through question 6 with them, pointing out that it is a mathematical question but still requires comprehension of the information contained within the passage and within the first sentence of the question itself – try to resist helping them any further!

Crufton House, Crufton, Somerset, TA21 0ZE

A unique country property with fine views and set in seven acres of grounds, Crufton House is situated close to the church in the popular village of Crufton. It was built approximately 150 years ago but has recently been updated and modernised to a very high standard by the present owners.

The property

Crufton House is offered in excellent decorative order throughout. It enjoys the benefits of full oil-fired central heating via radiators and with some underfloor heating on the ground floor. The attractive stone-faced building comprises:

Spacious entrance hall with stone tiled flooring and oak staircase leading to galleried landing. Arched doorway to cloakroom with WC, wash-hand basin and fitted wardrobe.

Full length living room (7.5m by 4.8m) with large bay window offering fine views of Crufton Church and rear French doors leading to the outdoor paved area.

Dining room (6m by 4.8m) with fitted oak dresser.

Kitchen (5.2m by 4.6m), featuring a range of oak units incorporating a Belfast sink.

Master Bedroom (7.5m by 4.8m) with walk-in wardrobe and en-suite shower room fitted with double sink, WC, bidet and large shower.

Bedroom 1 (5.2m by 4.6m) with en-suite shower room fitted with sink, WC, bidet and shower.

Bedroom 2 (4.6m by 4.2m) with en-suite fitted with WC and sink.

Bedroom 3 (4.6m by 4.2m) with en-suite fitted with WC and sink.

Bedroom 4 (3.6m by 3.2m) with en-suite fitted with WC and sink.

Family Bathroom (4.1m by 3.8m) with attractive suite comprising WC, sink, bath and shower in full-glazed unit.

Triple garage with adjoining workshop. Seven acres of gardens laid mainly to lawns and featuring a range of specimen trees, including lime, Turkey oak, Wellingtonia and Scots Pine.

Directions

From our office, follow the A92 towards Tunton. After three miles, turn left opposite the World View Inn, signposted Crufton. On entering the village the property can be found on the left hand side, adjacent to the church.

Viewings

Strictly by appointment through our office, on 01964 887766

Services

We believe that the property is served by mains gas, electricity, water and drainage. Please confirm this through the vendor and your solicitor.

Price

£1.2m freehold.

House for sale

Write full sentences to answer the questions.

1 What is the passage advertising?
   _____
   _____

2 How many bedrooms does the house have?
   _____
   _____

3 How many cars could fit in the garage?
   _____
   _____

4 What building can be seen from the lounge?
   _____
   _____

5 How old is the house?
   _____
   _____

6 How many toilets does the house have?
   _____
   _____

7 What trees does the garden have?
   _____
   _____

Notes for teachers
Help the children to read the passage slowly and carefully, ensuring that they understand that it consists of estate agents' details about a large house that is for sale. Do they remember to write in complete sentences, using appropriate punctuation? Discuss the meaning of 'WC' before the children attempt the questions.

House for sale

Name: _____ Date: _____

Imagine your own home is for sale. Write a set of estate agents' details advertising the property.

_____
_____
_____
_____
_____
_____
_____
_____
_____
_____
_____
_____
_____
_____
_____
_____
_____
_____
_____
_____
_____
_____
_____
_____

Notes for teachers
Ask the children to read the passage slowly carefully, ensuring that they understand that it consists of estate agents' details about a large house that is for sale. Provide them with the estate agents' details on the flat featured in the previous exercise. Encourage them to use both sets of details as prompts for their own writing.

House for sale

Name: _____ Date: _____

Read about the house for sale and re-read the estate agents' details about a flat for sale. Make comparisons between the two sets of details. Are there any similarities? What are the differences?

_____
_____
_____
_____
_____
_____
_____
_____
_____
_____
_____
_____
_____
_____
_____
_____
_____
_____
_____
_____
_____
_____
_____
_____

Notes for teachers
Ask the children to read the passage slowly carefully, ensuring that they understand that it consists of estate agents' details about a large house that is for sale. Provide them with the estate agents' details on the flat featured in the previous exercise.

Running for his life

The passage below is an extract from 'Wolf Brother' by Michelle Paver, the first book in the 'Chronicles of Ancient Darkness' series.

Torak crashed through alder thickets and sank to his knees in bogs. Birch trees whispered of his passing. Silently he begged them not to tell the bear.

The wound in his arm burned, and with each breath his bruised ribs ached savagely, but he didn't dare stop. The Forest was full of eyes. He pictured the bear coming after him. He ran on.

He startled a young boar grubbing up pignuts, and grunted a quick apology to ward off an attack. The boar gave an ill-tempered snort and let him pass.

A wolverine snarled at him to stay away, and he snarled back as fiercely as he could, because wolverines only listen to threats. The wolverine decided he meant it, and shot up a tree.

To the east, the sky was wolf grey. Thunder growled. In the stormy light, the trees were a brilliant green. Rain in the mountains, thought Torak numbly. Watch out for flash floods.

He forced himself to think of that – to push away the horror. It didn't work. He ran on.

At last he had to stop for breath. He collapsed against an oak tree. As he raised his head to stare at the shifting green leaves, the tree murmured secrets to itself, shutting him out.

For the first time in his life he was truly alone. He didn't feel part of the Forest any more. He felt as if his world-soul had snapped its link to all other living things: tree and bird, hunter and prey, river and rock. Nothing in the whole world knew how he felt. Nothing wanted to know.

Running for his life

Write complete sentences to answer the questions below.

1 From what book is this passage taken?

2 What is Torak running away from?

3 How is Torak injured?

4 Three different types of trees are mentioned in the passage. What are they?

5 What problem could rain in the mountains cause?

6 Which animals did Torak meet and how did he avoid them attacking him?

Notes for teachers
Help the children to read the passage slowly and carefully, ensuring that they understand the story. Discuss the questions with them and encourage them to work out their answers orally before putting anything down on paper. Do they remember to write in complete sentences, using appropriate punctuation?

Running for his life

Write complete sentences to answer the questions below.

1. Who is the author of the passage?

2. What does the word 'chronicles' mean?

3. What did Torak think could be dangerous about the birch trees?

4. Why didn't Torak dare stop?

5. What is a wolverine?

6. In what way do you think 'the Forest was full of eyes'? How do you think Torak felt about the Forest?

Notes for teachers
Ask the children to read the passage carefully, ensuring that they understand the story. Discuss the questions with them and encourage them to work out their answers orally before putting anything down on paper. They may need to use a dictionary to help them to answer questions 2 and 5. Do they remember to write in complete sentences, using appropriate punctuation?

Running for his life

Write complete sentences to answer the questions below.

1. Which danger frightened Torak the most?

2. Why do you think the writer described the sky as 'wolf grey' and stated that the thunder 'growled'?

3. What do you think that Torak felt about trees?

4. There are eight paragraphs in the passage. Most of them mention at least one danger facing Torak. List all the dangers that are mentioned.

5. Describe the range of feelings that Torak experienced.

6. **On a separate piece of paper write your own story about running from dangers.**

Notes for teachers
Ask the children to read the passage carefully, ensuring that they understand the story. Discuss the questions with them and encourage them to work out their answers orally before putting anything down on paper. Do they remember to write in complete sentences, using appropriate punctuation? Talk about the final task – the pupils may wish to use a setting they know well, considering what dangers may face them. The passage should give them clues as to style and pace.

Wolf

In the book 'Wolf Brother' by Michelle Paver, the young boy Torak befriends a most unusual companion, a wolf cub. The passage below gives information about wolves.

The wolf (Latin name *Canis Lupus*) is a large, powerful carnivorous mammal.

Grey wolves live in small packs consisting of a senior adult pair and their offspring, though sometimes the pair will 'adopt' other immature wolves. Each pack establishes a clear territory in which the pack members hunt for prey, constantly travelling but remaining within their chosen area. They avoid crossing out of their territory as they would be attacked by the wolf packs that occupy the neighbouring areas.

Wolves communicate with each other by howling. It is thought that they may howl for several purposes: to call the members of the pack together; to sound an alarm to other members of the pack if there is danger near their den; or to find each other.

Wolves feed mainly on large animals such as deer, moose, caribou, elk, wild boar and mountain sheep but they will also eat smaller animals and birds. As an extra component of their diet they may eat berries and fruit when these are in season.

On rare occasions wolves will attack people, though they are very cautious of humans and will avoid them whenever possible. Fear of wolves by humans has given rise to folk tales such as Little Red Riding Hood and the Three Little Pigs.

At one time wolves were common in some parts of Europe, Asia, Africa and North America but now there are much smaller numbers of wolves in these areas. Two hundred years ago wolves were widespread across mainland Europe but they were hunted by humans and exterminated from most countries. Small numbers of wolves still live in Spain, Italy and Finland but there are larger numbers in eastern Europe in countries such as Poland, Bulgaria and Romania. Wolves have not lived in the wild in this country since around the year 1500.

It seems incredible that the grey wolf is the main ancestor of the domestic dog. Even tiny dogs such as Yorkshire Terriers and Dachshunds are descended from the wild wolves that roamed the forests and moors thousands of years ago.

Wolf

Name: _____ Date: _____

Ring the correct answer for each of the following three questions.

1 A word meaning 'flesh-eating' is

      powerful   carnivorous   mammal   prey

2 A word similar in meaning to 'alarm' is

      warning   bell   burglar   howl

3 Another word for 'roamed' could be

      visited   lived   preyed   wandered

Use full sentences to answer the next questions.

4 In which language are the words *Canis Lupus* written?

_____

_____

5 What do wolves eat?

_____

_____

_____

6 Write how you feel about wolves.

_____

_____

_____

_____

_____

Notes for teachers
The pupils could complete this work after completing the comprehension 'Running for his life'. Help the children to read the passage slowly and carefully, ensuring that they understand that it is a non-fiction information text. Do they remember to write in complete sentences, using appropriate punctuation, for the final three questions? Talk about question 6, encouraging the children to consider whether they like wolves and whether they find them frightening, and to explain their feelings.

Wolf

Name: _____ Date: _____

Ring the correct answer for each of the following three questions.

1 A word meaning the area of land that the wolves occupy is

      component   parts   widespread   territory

2 A word similar in meaning to 'component' is

      area   part   piece   food

3 Another word for 'cautious' could be

      careful   nervous   caution   frightened

Use full sentences to answer the next questions.

4 Describe what is meant by a 'pack' of wolves.

_____
_____
_____

5 Why do you think wolves establish a territory? What would happen if other wolves came into their territory?

_____
_____
_____
_____

6 What similarities do domestic dogs have to wolves?

_____
_____
_____
_____
_____

Notes for teachers
The pupils could complete this work after completing the comprehension 'Running for his life'. Ask the children to read the passage carefully, ensuring that they understand that it is a non-fiction information text. For the first three questions, ensure that they consider the words in the context of the passage. Do they remember to write in complete sentences, using appropriate punctuation, for the final three questions? Talk about question 6, encouraging the children to think about what dogs eat, the sounds they make and their appearance.

Wolf

1 **Read the passage carefully then read each paragraph again. Write a brief statement regarding the purpose of each paragraph. The first two are completed for you.**

Paragraph 1 gives a brief explanation of the type of animal that a wolf is.

Paragraph 2 explains the social interactions of wolves.

Paragraph 3
_____
_____

Paragraph 4
_____
_____

Paragraph 5
_____
_____

Paragraph 6
_____
_____

Paragraph 7
_____
_____

Notes for teachers
The pupils could complete this work after completing the comprehension 'Running for his life'. Ask the children to read the passage carefully, ensuring that they understand that it is a non-fiction information text. Encourage them to write as little as possible to explain each paragraph. An extension activity would be for the pupils to write about another animal following most of the structure used in the text about wolves.

Lone Dog

I'm a lean dog, a keen dog, a wild dog and lone,
I'm a rough dog, a tough dog, hunting on my own!
I'm a bad dog, a mad dog, teasing silly sheep;
I love to sit and bay at the moon and keep fat souls from sleep.

I'll never be a lap dog, licking dirty feet,
A sleek dog, a meek dog, cringing for my meat.
Not for me the fireside, the well-filled plate,
But shut the door and sharp stone and cuff and kick and hate.

Not for me the other dogs, running by my side,
Some have run a short while, but none of them would bide.
O mine is still the lone trail, the hard trail, the best,
Wide wind and wild stars and the hunger of the quest.

by Irene McLeod

Lone Dog

Name: _____ Date: _____

Read 'Lone Dog' then answer the questions using your best handwriting.

1 What type of passage is this piece of writing?
   _____
   _____

2 Write the pairs of words that rhyme with each other in the first verse.
   _____   _____
   _____   _____
   _____   _____
   _____   _____
   _____   _____

3 How does the dog keep people awake at night?
   _____
   _____

4 Does the dog live with other dogs? How do you know?
   _____
   _____

5 Does the dog live with people? How do you know?
   _____
   _____

6 Would you like to have this dog as a pet? Explain your answer.
   _____
   _____
   _____
   _____
   _____

Notes for teachers
Help the children to read the passage slowly and carefully, ensuring that they understand that it consists of a rhyming poem. Discuss the questions with them and encourage them to work out their answers orally before putting anything down on paper. Do they remember to write in complete sentences, using appropriate punctuation?

Lone Dog

Name: _____ Date: _____

Read 'Lone Dog' then answer the questions using your best handwriting.

1 Briefly describe the structure of the poem.
   _____
   _____

2 Write the pairs of words that rhyme with each other in the second verse.

   _____   _____
   _____   _____
   _____   _____
   _____   _____
   _____   _____

3 How do you think the dog finds food?
   _____
   _____

4 What does the dog despise about the life of a domestic dog?
   _____
   _____

5 Has the dog had the company of other dogs? What happened?
   _____
   _____

6 Write a short description of the dog's way of life.
   _____
   _____
   _____
   _____

Notes for teachers
Ask the children to read the passage carefully, ensuring that they understand that it consists of a rhyming poem. Discuss the questions with them and encourage them to work out their answers before putting anything down on paper. Do they remember to write in complete sentences, using appropriate punctuation?

Andrew Brodie: More Improving Comprehension for Ages 10–11 © A&C Black, Bloomsbury Publishing 2012

Lone Dog

Read 'Lone Dog' then answer the questions using your best handwriting.

1. The poem includes two rhyming patterns within the first two verses. Describe these rhyming patterns.

2. In what way is the third verse different to the first two verses?

3. Do you think that this dog is a wolf? Find evidence from the poem that could support this idea and further evidence that could disprove it.

4. Write a four line verse about this dog or about an animal of your choice.

Notes for teachers
Ask the children to read the passage carefully, ensuring that they understand that it consists of a rhyming poem. Encourage them to explain the evidence they find. Do they remember to write in complete sentences, using appropriate punctuation?

William Shakespeare

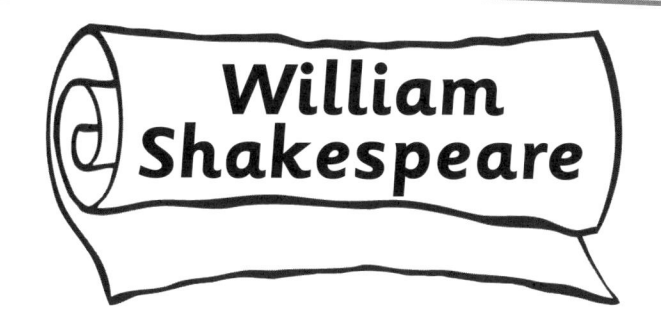

William Shakespeare is one of the most famous people who ever lived, as his poems and plays are known throughout the world. At least one of his plays is almost certainly still being produced somewhere in the world every day of the year, except perhaps Christmas Day.

Shakespeare was born in Stratford-upon-Avon in 1564. His father was John Shakespeare and his mother's maiden name was Mary Arden. Nobody knows William's exact date of birth but he was baptised on 26th April – some people assume that he was born just a few days before, on 23rd April. If that is true, Shakespeare would have been exactly fifty-two years old when he died on 23rd April in 1616.

William married Anne Hathaway when he was only eighteen years old and together they had three children. Their first child was called Susanna, who was born in 1583. Nearly two years later, Anne gave birth to twins, a boy called Hamnet and a girl, Judith. Sadly, Hamnet died when he was eleven years old.

When he was still in his twenties, Shakespeare's plays started to be performed in London. Shakespeare was frequently one of the actors in his own plays. He formed a company along with some of the other players and they built their own theatre alongside the River Thames. The Globe Theatre was constructed in 1599 but was burned down just fourteen years later. A modern replica of the Globe was built, very close to the original site, in 1997.

Shakespeare's plays include histories such as *Richard II*, *Henry IV* parts 1 and 2, *Henry V*, *Henry VI* parts 1, 2 and 3, *Richard III* and *Henry VIII*. He also wrote comedies such as *A Midsummer Night's Dream*, tragedies such as *Macbeth* and tragicomedies such as *The Tempest*. One of his most famous plays is *Romeo and Juliet*, the story of two young people who fell in love despite the fact that their families were enemies of each other. The play ends with the tragic death of the couple.

William Shakespeare

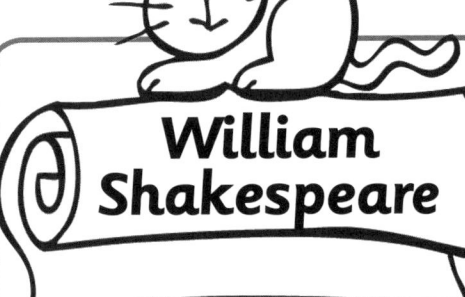

Ring the correct answer for each of the first three questions.

1   William Shakespeare was a famous

      playwright   wheelwright   shipwright   actor

2   A word similar in meaning to 'well-known' is

      celebrity   celebrate   famously   famous

3   Another word for 'produced' could be

      manufactured   presented   cooked   prepared

Use full sentences to answer the next questions.

4   What was Shakespeare's mother's surname before she married?

5   How old was Shakespeare when the first Globe Theatre was built?

6   Write the titles of five of Shakespeare's plays.

Notes for teachers
Help the children to read the passage slowly and carefully, ensuring that they understand that it is a non-fiction information text. Encourage them to answer the first three questions by considering the words in the context of the passage.

William Shakespeare

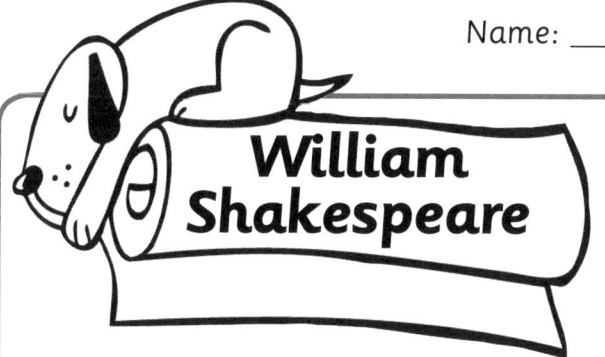

Ring the best answer for each of the first three questions.

1. William Shakespeare was born in

    1997   1616   1583   1564

2. A word similar in meaning to 'performed' is

    acted   presented   danced   sung

3. Another word for 'frequently' could be

    sometimes   never   occasionally   often

Use full sentences to answer the next questions.

4. How old was Shakespeare when his first daughter was born?
   _____
   _____

5. In what year did Hamnet die?
   _____
   _____

6. In what year did the first Globe Theatre burn down?
   _____
   _____

7. In which romantic play did the title characters die?
   _____
   _____

Notes for teachers
Ask the children to read the passage carefully, ensuring that they understand that it is a non-fiction information text. Encourage them to answer each of the first three questions by considering the words in the context of the passage – more than one answer could be correct but the pupils should choose the most suitable.

Name: _____ Date: _____

William Shakespeare

Ring the best answer for each of the first three questions.

1 William Shakespeare died in

      1997   1616   1583   1564

2 A word similar in meaning to 'actor' is

      performer   playwright   player   producer

3 Another word for 'sad' could be

      tragic   sorry   vicious   violent

Use full sentences to answer the next questions.

4 In what town was Shakespeare born?

_____

_____

5 Where was the Globe Theatre built?

_____

_____

6 Give an example of each type of play by William Shakespeare: tragedy, history and comedy.

_____

_____

_____

7 Find out about the Scottish king, called Macbeth. When did he become king and when did he die?

_____

_____

_____

Notes for teachers
Ask the children to read the passage carefully, ensuring that they understand that it is a non-fiction information text. Encourage them to answer each of the first three questions by considering the words in the context of the passage – more than one answer could be correct but the pupils should choose the most suitable. For the final question the children will need to research the internet.

Macbeth

The extract below is from Murder at Dunsinane, a short story contained in the book The Enchanted Island by Ian Serraillier. Murder at Dunsinane is a retelling of Shakespeare's tragic play Macbeth.

It was a day of mingled storm and sunshine, with dark scudding clouds and torrential bursts of rain. Two Scottish generals, Macbeth and Banquo, were riding home from battle to report a great victory. They had just defeated a rebel army that had risen up against King Duncan of Scotland, whose kingdom in those ancient times was separate from England. Macbeth in particular had shown amazing courage. Brandishing his sword, he had carved his way through the enemy ranks till he stood face to face with their leader. Then with one tremendous blow he had cut his body in two.

As the two generals were galloping over a wind-lashed desolate moor, suddenly there was a flash of lightning and a clap of thunder. Three weird and ragged figures – like creatures from another world – sprang in front of the horses. They had withered skins, wild glittering eyes, and except for their beards were more like women than men.

'Who are you and what do you want with us?' cried Banquo, reining in his horse.

While the rain streamed down their faces, they pressed their choppy forefingers against their skinny lips, to show that they would answer no questions. They were witches.

'Speak if you can. What are you?' cried Macbeth, as his horse champed and snorted, its hot flanks streaming.

'All hail Macbeth, Thane of Glamis!' cried the first witch.

'All hail Macbeth, Thane of Cawdor!' cried the second witch.

Macbeth was startled. How could he hold that title when the Thane of Cawdor was still alive?

'All hail Macbeth!' cried the third witch. 'Soon you will be King of Scotland.'

Stirred to his very soul, Macbeth lifted his hand to hide his eyes. Strange thoughts that he did not wholly understand had begun to stir in his brain. Who were these creatures and what did they intend? Were they bringing him some message from the powers beyond life? If so, was it good or evil?

Macbeth

Name: _____ Date: _____

Write complete sentences to answer these questions.

1 From which short story is the passage taken?
_____
_____

2 What book is the short story in?
_____
_____

3 What were the names of the two Scottish generals?
_____
_____

4 Where were the two generals?
_____
_____

5 Who jumped out in front of the two men?
_____
_____

6 What strange prophecy did the three women tell Macbeth?
_____
_____

7 How do you think Macbeth felt about the prophecy?
_____
_____

Notes for teachers
Help the children to read the passage slowly and carefully, ensuring that they understand that this is a passage taken from a retelling of Shakespeare's Macbeth. Discuss the questions with them and encourage them to work out their answers orally before putting anything down on paper. The final question is particularly challenging and will need some discussion.

Macbeth

Name: _____ Date: _____

Write complete sentences to answer these questions.

1 Who wrote 'The Enchanted Island'?
   _____
   _____

2 Describe the weather on the day when the story is set.
   _____
   _____
   _____

3 What was the nationality of the two generals?
   _____
   _____

4 Where had the two generals been?
   _____
   _____

5 The witches made two prophecies. What was the first prophecy?
   _____
   _____

6 Why was Macbeth shocked to hear the first prophecy?
   _____
   _____

7 What is a 'Thane'?
   _____
   _____

Notes for teachers
Ask the children to read the passage carefully, ensuring that they understand that this is a passage taken from a retelling of Shakespeare's Macbeth. Discuss the questions with them and encourage them to work out their answers orally before putting anything down on paper. The final question will require the pupils to make some research.

Andrew Brodie: More Improving Comprehension for Ages 10–11 © A&C Black, Bloomsbury Publishing 2012

Macbeth

Write complete sentences to answer these questions.

1 Who wrote 'Murder at Dunsinane'?

2 From what were Macbeth and Banquo returning?

3 Who were the two men fighting for?

4 Describe the three witches.

5 What two prophecies did the witches make to Macbeth?

6 How do you think Banquo felt about the prophecies?

7 Research Glamis and Cawdor. Find out where they are. Find out what special buildings are in both places.

Notes for teachers
Ask the children to read the passage carefully, ensuring that they understand that this is a passage taken from a retelling of Shakespeare's Macbeth. Discuss the questions with them and encourage them to work out their answers orally before putting anything down on paper. The final question requires internet research – do the children find any reference to Macbeth in their research?

Snowmen

A sketch for three characters.

Two snowmen are talking to each other.

A   Hello.

B   Hello.

A   You're new round here, aren't you?

B   We all are!

A   I suppose that's true. Snow only came yesterday morning so I was born yesterday afternoon.

B   So was I! That means we've got the same birthday!

A   Yes, I saw you being made.

B   So you're a bit older than me.

A   That's right. Lovely weather we're having!

B   Yes, I love it! Really cold but a bit of sunshine just to brighten up the day.

A   I've heard it's going to snow again later.

B   Really? That's great news!

A   Yes, it certainly is because there'll probably be more of us after that.

B   We'll be able to have a party.

A   Hey, watch out! Someone's coming.

B   Who is it?

A   It's the girl who made you. Keep still and don't say a word!

B   OK.

C   Hello Snowman, you look wonderful!

B   Thank you!

C   AAH! *She runs away.*

Snowmen

Write complete sentences to answer the questions.

1 How many characters speak in this script?

2 Who are the two main characters?

3 What was the weather like on the day before this story is set?

4 What is the weather like on the day the story is set?

5 Who came to see the two snowmen?

6 Why did she run away?

Notes for teachers
After the seriousness of Macbeth, this passage is a light-hearted script. As with all play scripts it provides the opportunity for pupils to read and re-read by taking turns at each of the three parts. They may wish to give names to the characters. Do they remember to write their answers to the questions in complete sentences, using appropriate punctuation?

Snowmen

Write complete sentences to answer the questions.

1 Why are the two main characters 'new round here'?
   _____
   _____

2 On what day were the two main characters born?
   _____
   _____

3 Why is one character older than the other?
   _____
   _____

4 Why does the weather suit the two characters well?
   _____
   _____

5 Why did one character tell the other one to keep still and to keep quiet?
   _____
   _____

6 Why did the girl run away?
   _____
   _____

7 What could happen next?
   _____
   _____

Notes for teachers
After the seriousness of Macbeth, this passage is a light-hearted script. As with all play scripts it provides the opportunity for pupils to read and re-read by taking turns at each of the three parts. They may wish to give names to the characters. Do they remember to write their answers to the questions in complete sentences, using appropriate punctuation?

Snowmen

Name: _____ Date: _____

Write complete sentences to answer the questions.

1 Why are all the snowmen 'new round here'?
_____
_____

2 Describe the weather over the two days of the story.
_____
_____
_____
_____

3 Why will the snowmen be able to have a party?
_____
_____

4 Why did the girl run away?
_____
_____

5 What could happen next? Write a continuation of the sketch.
_____
_____
_____
_____
_____
_____
_____
_____
_____

Notes for teachers
After the seriousness of Macbeth, this passage is a light-hearted script. As with all play scripts it provides the opportunity for pupils to read and re-read by taking turns at each of the three parts. They may wish to give names to the characters. Do they remember to write their answers to the questions in complete sentences, using appropriate punctuation?

Football practice 1

1. It's football practice after school
   My friends all think it's great.
   I'm worried that I'll look a fool,
   Can't back out now – too late.

2. My mum, she says I have to go,
   While she is out at work.
   A thousand times I've told her 'no'
   'Cos I look such a jerk.

3. I don't know what is wrong with me,
   I just can't kick the ball.
   There's places I would rather be,
   But I can't escape at all.

4. When it's time to pick the team
   I'm always chosen last.
   The other players never seem
   To forget my dreadful past.

5. I had to go in goal one day
   The ball came straight to me.
   Trouble is, the way I play,
   I knocked it with my knee.

6. It bounced just once then hit the net,
   A goal! That was my dream,
   But why did I just have to get
   The goal for the other team?

7. Thank goodness that game's over now
   I'd like to start afresh.
   I still have dreams about just how
   My goal would hit the mesh.

8. So here I am, stood in the cold,
   My legs have turned to jelly.
   The ball's in play, to me it's rolled,
   And their goalie's on his belly!

Name: _____ Date: _____

Football practice 1

Write full sentences to answer the questions. Check your punctuation carefully.

1 What type of text is this?
_____
_____

2 What is happening after school?
_____
_____

3 Why is the writer worried about it?
_____
_____

4 Why does the writer's mum want him to go to football practice?
_____
_____

5 What was wrong with the last goal that the writer scored?
_____
_____

6 Write about a time when you had to do something that you did not want to do.
_____
_____
_____
_____

Notes for teachers
Help the children to read the poem slowly and carefully, ensuring that they understand the sequence of events. Discuss the questions with them and encourage them to work out their answers orally before putting anything down on paper. Do they remember to write in complete sentences, using appropriate punctuation?

58   Andrew Brodie: More Improving Comprehension for Ages 10–11 © A&C Black, Bloomsbury Publishing 2012

Football practice 1

Write full sentences to answer the questions. Check your punctuation carefully.

1 Describe the rhyme structure of this poem.

2 What do the writer's friends think about football practice?

3 In what ways are the writer's friends not kind to him?

4 What happened on the occasion that nobody seems able to forget?

5 What would the writer like to happen?

6 Write about a sporting event that you have taken part in.

Notes for teachers
Ask the children to read the poem carefully, ensuring that they understand the sequence of events. Can they identify the rhyming pattern? Encourage them to consider the number of lines in each verse and to observe where the rhymes occur. Do they remember to write in complete sentences, using appropriate punctuation?

Football practice 1

Write full sentences to answer the questions. Check your punctuation carefully.

1 Describe the structure of this poem.

2 Has the writer really told his mum 'no' a thousand times? Explain why he said he had.

3 What evidence do we have that the writer is not very good at football?

4 What dreams does the writer have?

5 Describe what is good and what is not so good about the situation for the writer in verse 8?

6 Write about your dream. What would you like to happen for you?

Notes for teachers
Ask the children to read the poem carefully, ensuring that they understand the sequence of events. Can they identify the pattern of the poem? Encourage them to observe the number of verses, the length of each verse and the rhyming pattern in each verse. Do they remember to write in complete sentences, using appropriate punctuation?

60   Andrew Brodie: More Improving Comprehension for Ages 10–11 © A&C Black, Bloomsbury Publishing 2012

Football practice 2

9   This is my chance, I start to run
    And dribble with the ball.
    And suddenly I'm having fun
    It's not so bad at all.

10 I dodge one player, and the rest
    There's only one boy more.
    I've got the ball, I'll do my best,
    There is a chance I'll score!

11 I bring my foot back, bend my leg,
    Then give the ball a whack,
    I'm on my knees, I start to beg,
    But fears come flooding back.

12 Their goalie's up, he's on his feet,
    And running out to save.
    His skilful hands are hard to beat,
    There's no-one else so brave.

13 Time stands still, it's silent now,
    And look the goalie dives.
    He looks surprised, at how, just how,
    My bending shot arrives.

14 The ball it knocks him to the ground,
    But it's not finished yet.
    And as he turns to look around
    The ball is in the net!

15 I've got my goal, my dream's come true,
    My friends all gather near.
    And suddenly from all their mouths
    I hear a great big cheer.

16 It's football practice after school
    My friends all think it's great.
    They also think that I'm so cool,
    Mind out … I can't be late.

Name: _____ Date: _____

Football practice 2

Write full sentences to answer the questions. Check your punctuation carefully.

1 What is the rhyme structure of the poem?
   _____
   _____

2 Why has the writer suddenly got a chance?
   _____
   _____

3 Which word tells us how the writer passes the players on the opposing team?
   _____
   _____

4 Why does the goalie look surprised?
   _____
   _____

5 What does the ball do to the goalie?
   _____
   _____

6 Write about a time when something great happened to you.
   _____
   _____
   _____
   _____
   _____

Notes for teachers
This comprehension should be completed after pupils have already worked on 'Football Practice 1'. Help the children to read the poem slowly and carefully, ensuring that they understand the sequence of events. Can they identify the rhyming pattern? Encourage them to consider the number of lines in each verse and to observe where the rhymes occur. Do they remember to write their answers to the questions in complete sentences, using appropriate punctuation?

Football practice 2

Name: _____ Date: _____

Write full sentences to answer the questions. Check your punctuation carefully.

1 Describe the structure of this poem.
_____
_____
_____

2 Why is the writer suddenly having fun?
_____
_____

3 How do the writer's friends react to his goal?
_____
_____

4 How does the writer feel about football practice now?
_____
_____

5 Describe the sequence of events in verses 9 to 15.
_____
_____
_____
_____
_____

6 Write a four-line verse about your own dream event.
_____
_____
_____
_____

Notes for teachers
This comprehension should be completed after pupils have already worked on 'Football Practice 1'. Ask the children to read the poem carefully, ensuring that they understand the sequence of events. Can they identify the pattern of the poem? Encourage them to observe the number of verses, the length of each verse and the rhyming pattern in each verse. Do they remember to write their answers to the questions in complete sentences, using appropriate punctuation?

Andrew Brodie: More Improving Comprehension for Ages 10–11 © A&C Black, Bloomsbury Publishing 2012

Football practice 2

1. Describe the sequence of events in the two parts of the poem 'Football Practice'.

2. Write a short poem, of similar structure to 'Football Practice', about an event that has happened to you.

Notes for teachers
This comprehension should be completed after pupils have already worked on 'Football Practice 1'. Ask the children to read the poem carefully, ensuring that they understand the sequence of events.